Mrs. Gurney's A

In justification of Mrs. ——'s friendship

Mary Jary Gurney

Alpha Editions

This edition published in 2023

ISBN : 9789357958851

Design and Setting By
Alpha Editions
www.alphaedis.com
Email - info@alphaedis.com

Contents

PREFACE.

In presenting to the world the extraordinary document which follows, the Publisher deems it fit, by way of Preface, to advert briefly to the principal circumstances and persons connected with this great outrage, which it embodies, upon the sensibilities and morals of the public—distinctly repudiating, himself, any endorsement of the views of the misguided writer, and deeply regretting the scandal which has attached in consequence of her acts to the influential Society of Friends, and to the numerous high families, with which she is allied, both in England and America.

The Gurney Family is known wherever on the Eastern or Western continent, philanthropy, charity, liberality in its most comprehensive meaning, scholarship and literary ability of the highest order, or wealth in the most profuse exuberance, becomes the theme of the social circle or the text of the author's pen. It is, moreover, one of the most notable and ancient of the English aristocracy, dating from the time of the Conqueror, ever since when they have held wealth and position in the County of Norfolk, where nearly all the various members of the name still reside. In England's early and stormy days they rendered essential service to the State in many famous battles both at home and abroad—for it was at a comparatively recent date only that this till then redoubtable race became identified, through some of its branches, with the pacific and lowly doctrines of the Quakers.

They are closely connected with families here of the very highest respectability of character—the celebrated John Joseph Gurney having taken a wife from this city; and no man in the Society of Friends ranked equal to him in his day, either in religious influence, mental ability, or excellence of heart. His indeed gave the name to the Gurneyite Orthodox Friends, of which branch of that sect he was the acknowledged leader. He died about twelve years ago.

His only son, John Henry Gurney, who was the heir not merely of his father's wealth, and name, but of his good character, is the betrayed husband of this story. He is the present representative in Parliament of King's Lynn, Norfolkshire, and is noted for his liberal political sentiments. He is now forty years of age.

His wife, Mary Gurney, the author of this letter, was the daughter and only child of Richard Hanbury Gurney, a first cousin of John Joseph, and belonging to the elder, wealthier, and representative branch of the race—he, Richard, deceased only within a few years, having been a younger half-brother, and the only one, of the actual head of the Family—the venerable Hudson Gurney, of Keswick, F.R.S., F.A.S., Ex-High Sheriff of Norfolk, etc., etc.

Whilst Hudson Gurney it is true inherited principally the patrimonial estates, Richard, his half-brother, became the heir of his own mother, who had been a Miss Hanbury of the wealthy family of London brewers of that name. This fortune, over a million sterling, became at Richard's death the inheritance of his daughter Mary, the author of this letter, now about twenty-eight years of age, and the mother of two or three children.

Samuel Gurney the eminent banker and philanthropist was a brother of John Joseph, and Mrs. Elizabeth Fry, whose labors and sacrifices to improve the discipline of the great prisons on both continents have won her a name to be envied, was his sister. Another sister was the wife, and zealous assistant, of Sir Thomas Fowell Buxton, celebrated in the annals of British Emancipation.

Mrs. Gurney is thus allied by descent and marriage with families of the first note both in Europe and America, and holds in her own right an almost princely estate. She was constantly, up to the very period of her departure, anticipated in her lightest wish by a husband who knew no will but her own. With such surroundings, elevating her to the very highest sphere of English social life, with all its splendors and attractions, and securing to her the enjoyment of every rational pleasure, after thirteen years of married life, she voluntarily renounced her husband, her children and family, not in any moment of passion, but through a calm conviction of reason, as she herself states, and left England, the mistress of a common groom from her stables.

There can be no pardon nor extenuation for this great social crime.

But the motives which led to it are well worthy of the reader's patient consideration. They are stated in her letter with logical precision, and at the same time with the apparent enthusiasm and tenderness of a heart which had suffered and loved intensely; and whatever the explanation, whether deducible from an exaggeration of facts, or an artful use of language, her words really seem to be stamped with the seal of social martyrdom.

Whilst the general tenor of the doctrines she enunciates cannot fail to administer a shock to every healthy mind, it is not necessary for the cause of morality, and it would be unjust indeed, to denounce her letter *in toto*.

Every authentic history of personal experience forms a helpful addition for the guidance and behavior of mankind.

The deplorable consequences of an early and hasty marriage, as portrayed in her own history, may serve as a useful beacon to rash youth in all ages to come.

Her earnest plea on behalf of Personal Merit cannot fail to win its way to many hearts—at least in this Country, the foster-home of the plebeiance and of democracy.

But to her concluding argument especially are attention and respect due.

The investigations heretofore made in this Country and Europe have developed a frightful catalogue of diseases and deaths resulting from inter-marriages; and more recent examinations in the wards of Hospitals, in the Asylums for Feeble-minded Children, in Institutions for the Deaf and Dumb, and Blind, trace directly those monstrosities and defects of organization, in a preponderating number of cases, to marriages of this character. Whether her immediate example furnished any confirmation on this head, the meagre details of the whole affair, which have been permitted to be divulged, do not afford any certain information; that it has been so in other branches of her family, and that the dread of it was upon her own mind, is most apparent in her letter.

Her authoritative and vehement invective against these internecine marriages, it cannot be doubted, will draw prominent attention to the subject; and on this account, and many others, some of which have been indicated, Mrs. Gurney's Letter requires at least no "apology" for being made public.

MRS. GURNEY'S APOLOGY.

PARIS, *January* —, 1860.

DEAR E * * *:

Your name has been always on my lips and in my heart, and you alone of all the world have never questioned me. I come to you again, E * * *, as I have so often—as I did when we were children, when you folded me trustfully in your arms—and say to you: I am as I was then; and I hear you say: Tell me nothing, for I believe you always, and there must be no questioning between us.

What I shall write to you will not be to cast a doubt upon our perfect and entire sympathy by any explanation, but to fulfil what I feel to be a duty towards you—to put you in possession of all that may weigh in the least degree with those at all understanding my nature, before whom you care to justify your steadfast attachment to me, though the performance of this duty, dear E * * *, may impose upon me the revelation of my inmost life. If, in your judgment, there will be here presented aught of such justification, show it to them, wholly or partially, just as you think well, remembering that this is for your sake, not my own. My justification it would be needful to make before a much wider tribunal, for I have perpetrated an act which the whole conventional world have leagued together, in ignorance, prejudice and hypocrisy, to denominate a crime, and I could expect little or no sympathy from that wide bar of public judgment that knows nothing of me nor of my surroundings, and which never could be made to comprehend my nature; or, comprehending it, would not even then, at this day, be prepared to accept any argument or explanation in extenuation of my course.

E * * *, you remember me at fourteen; you remember the time we returned from the visit to Wymondham; you remember how, repulsing the cold influences overcoming me in spite of myself, I dashed down in the carriage the plain bonnet they had asked me to wear that day, and stamped on it, and let all my hair fall down upon my shoulders, and said: I am free. You remember it well. And then, at last, when the carriage reached the house, how we threw ourselves into each other's arms, and I had no more courage, and feared to avow the act, telling them you sat down on it—and you were still; and then how I cried all night, that I denied the truth of my nature—that I was not free.

E * * *, that day repeated itself through my life—in every act, in the worship of God, in my marriage, in the very conception of my children; and I looked forward to its last repetition only in my death.

It is past now—my living death is over. I have chosen between the universal condemnation of the world and my own sense of right; not in any sublime way, but in the simple, truthful way my nature craved. I lie down in the evening and rise in the morning, for the first time since a child, blessing God for my existence. Nothing can rob me of this now but death alone. I have that treasure to a woman's heart that a woman can alone understand—the open avowal of the love that controls her being. With it, part of it, all of it, is the man, free from prejudice, filled with every noble aspiration, who is its object. Should I, I ask you, have preferred the reputation which the world accords to her who, yielding to its forms, becomes daily the living lie it approves?

They who go on disposing of human instincts, human affections and human brains in their own way, according to their own sense of right and wrong, should go further; they should change their meeting-houses and churches into monasteries and convents, and watch the religious aspirations they would control by daily and nightly supervision. Into their homes they should introduce harem espionage, that the bodily instincts, which they hold in enforced compliance, may never have an opportunity to assert the truth about themselves.

Heresy and adultery, the two excommunicative words, which social life suspends over the doomed head of a woman who thinks and acts contrary to its rules of action, have not that full power and effect they are supposed to have. Nothing but actual physical imprisonment of the body, and, if it were possible, of the mind, can prevent a woman from becoming the secret avower of her belief and of her instincts. The excommunicative words do not restrain from either offence; they only develop that unquestionable vice of woman's weakness, hypocrisy.

The brain, when infidel, is infidel by its own proper organization, and they who assail its infidelity strike vainly at the God who made it, and implanted it in every newborn soul; the body, when infidel to the connection in which it is placed, is so by its own proper instincts, and they, who attempt to control it, strike, likewise, at a law of its creation.

When will narrow-minded, bigoted men learn that the one absolute, controlling law of a woman's nature is love—that it is the only good and desirable thing about a woman—the only reliable thing about her? They can trust her, with her love, to live in a house of prostitution; they cannot control her, without it, by the most absolute, social ostracism.

And this love, what is it? It is a power present always in the world, which, recognized by two like natures, thenceforth binds them to each other, beyond the control, and in violation, if need be, of any other law—as my mother's love bound her to my father, and my father's love bound him to her, and gave me my being—a being cradled in the tenderest, truest passion that ever existed between two human beings.

How long have I been in ascertaining and yielding myself up to this divine law! What wasted years! What subjections derogatory to the vilest nature! What hypocrisy, dishonoring to God! What suffering have I caused this man, assigned to me alone, since that day on which I first in him recognized myself!

It seems so long ago; it seems far longer to me than the time makes it; it seems as if an eternity had rolled backward to that day.

Oh, I had questionings of right and wrong in that fathomless interval of despair, far other, far deeper, than all I had been taught or could be taught by their lips—questionings that brought me to the very brink of death.

Why should I have loved him? Why do I love him? What is it I love in him? All this I have asked myself a thousand times, and there has never been, can never be, an answer to all this questioning.

Yet I say now to you: Why should I not love him? What is there not to love in him? My heart only answers: What is there in me that I should be loved, that I should know that joy which in its tiniest moment makes all years of other time a mockery?

And these questions do we ask each other daily and nightly forever.

And yet there is one reason, they say, why I should not have loved him— one word there is which the world places as an impassable barrier between us—a word that has never crossed my lips till now—a meaningless word, and yet involving in their eyes a crime as great as that adultery which I commit—just as great, for both are equally meaningless as touching our relation.

And that word expresses the social position he bore me. Rather than have been his lawful wife even, I might have been a king's mistress, or any nobleman's paramour, with less offence.

And I, who was the reputable bawd of marriage rites, was I above him? I, a daily offence against decency in obedience to the same social law that would have forced him to life-long humility? Was I above him? How? In what way? I, sunk, in the abasement of my own weak unnatural compliance, below the veriest nameless outcast? Could I be above anything? Was he not at least my peer? He, who, if we leave too such vapid questions of distinction, is Hyperion to a Satyr compared in person with me—short, fat, little body that I am!

I have silently asked myself in his arms, when I dared not soil our lips with their utterance, about these words—groom and adulterer. Yet well I knew that they had no relation to our love—that they were but words—that a true soul no social contamination defiles or degrades—that nobility unrecognized and virtue an outcast, wherever placed, are eternally the same.

I had learned these lessons from a parent's lips. The example of my own true-hearted mother had taught me this. My own life had been given me in violation of society's teachings.

Noble-hearted woman! who could say (I their child, and the only one that blessed at last their union, nearly a year old then:) Richard Gurney, I have withholden from you nothing; I have sacrificed all at the altar of love—even my little Marian—yet I ask no formal bond of union in return; I care not for it. What I had when our little one's life began—what I have now—what I know nothing can deprive me of now—your love—contents me. And he as nobly answered: Not for the sake of it, Mary, for it will have but little acknowledgment from my kindred or the world; but for the pride of the open avowal, and for the sake of our little girl, I marry you.

And this love, so true, so self-immolating, met, as he anticipated, with no approbation from his family. You remember how my husband, as an especial favor, asked Miss ——, and would solicit the members of his family, to accompany me to see my mother—a woman as far above them all in every instinct of her soul as was my father—the true representative of the Lords of Gournai and Le Braii.

Yet such was the affectation of superiority they always persevered in!

I know the world says we who are of English lineage never look so low to find high things.

This is not, and was never, true of me nor of my blood. I would, were it needful to find my ideal, as my father before me, search through any situation, just as men dig down for jewels; and I would have delved to the uttermost profound for that which I now possess. But he whom I loved was not so far; he was near me by the permission of that social law we have offended. The home of his family became established near my own. He was oft actually beside me, and separated only by that word from me; nay, he had right to touch me by permission of this social law—was charged temporarily with the safety of my life even—could speak to me, but respectfully— respectfully! He who was in reality of kindred blood, and made for me—for me—whom they paid court to, not because of the instinct of that blood, but because of the narrow thrift of my kinsmen.

But enough of this. I might have spared myself the contempt that tingles through my veins.

I loved him, E * * *; that was all. He became all I did, all I said, my very life. If I say more I may err, for I truly know no more, and shall never know more than this.

The whole scope and measure of a woman's heart and brain, and the whole purpose of her being, is love; and her whole knowledge forces itself into one inquiry: Am I worthy of the love of him I love? And does he love me? But I have thought over all this social matter, and have asked myself if I could have loved him better if he had not been what he was—if he had been a member of Parliament? Well, they had been plenty in our family—there were, among the rest, uncle Hudson, and cousin Charles, and cousin Edward Buxton, and cousin Priscilla's husband; so, too, father had consented to be; and finally, Jackey himself was there, and filling Walpole's chair, or at least the edge of it. And what was it but too palpable a sham? We all knew this—men and women—and we lived on it meanly, enjoying the empty honor and the empty praises of those in truth below us, because they so stupidly praised us. Oh, it was so foolish, all this member of Parliament pride! I loved William rather because he was not a member of Parliament—at least because it was not his aspiration. And then, if he had been an elder of the meeting? He!—what think you of that, E * * *? Or my Lord Bishop of Norwich—the Lord of diluted *pater nosters*—was he above him? Are these the things to marry a breathing woman to? Does any one think a *liaison* with the Bishop would have ennobled me?—or the embraces of the elder?

It is scarcely needful to say to you, my dear, that in the above there is not the slightest personal disrespect intended to Mr. Pelham or any other individual being.

True men are not such. A woman's instincts repel such forms of men. You may dress the real as meanly as an American slave, or you may elaborate the attire of the counterfeit to the antipodes of this—to pontifical robes—and the living soul of a woman will never fail to distinguish the false from the true.

Why you yourself, E * * *, would have wept your eyes out, I am sure, if I could have deliberately linked myself to the lifeless purpose in which the vitality of such beings ends.

He is not one of these. He is a man, E * * *, whom I love. Do you wonder I love him? It is because he is a man—a man, and not a hollow make-believe.

It is so with every true woman. In her love she recognizes no distinction of position. The gods of her idolatry, like the statues of the Greeks—whether standing in a rough warehouse or in the Louvre—remain unchanged in the calmness of their beauty and power. We ask nothing more of them but themselves, to gaze upon them, to become intoxicated, and to die with the love of them. Such seems to me the man to whom, by the profoundest law of my nature, I yield my being.

But will the world understand this? Perhaps it is the accident of my place and estate, that, surrounding me with what passes by the name of power, made me see its emptiness—that, uniting me to the highest representative of a religion in the person of a son who put it lightly off, made its meaningless character apparent—that, teaching me to strengthen a family distinction by the unconscious sacrifice of myself to him in whose control I had been somehow left, taught me to question if it were right, and at last to rise above and throw off the chains of an unnatural compliance.

My intercourse and secret correspondence with you from my early girlhood taught you how wayward, how passionate I was; and those letters are so much a part of me that I cannot write anything again as they were written.

You have preserved them; read them again, even to the days that followed my unnatural blood-kin union and its results.

Blood-kin union it was. Intermarriage always.

There was the marriage of my husband's uncle John with my aunt Elizabeth, first cousins.

Blood-kin union of my husband's father and mother, third cousins.

Intermarriage of my husband's uncle, Henry Birkbeck, with Jane Gurney, third cousins.

Intermarriage of my husband's father with Mary Fowler, cousin of his first wife.

Is it strange that such unions should prove unfortunate? Elizabeth Gurney and Jane Birkbeck only survived their marriages a year. Jane Gurney, my husband's mother, lived but four or five years of marriage life.

There, too, in the case of grandfather and aunt Agatha, was the anomaly of father and daughter marrying sister and brother.

There was the marriage of my husband's cousin Henry with Jane Birkbeck, his second cousin.

Then came the marriage of Catharine Gurney with her first cousin, Edward Buxton.

Then Rachel with Thomas Buxton, another pair of first cousins.

About a year thence, after the interesting grief on his part at the death of his aunt Fry, our uncle Buxton, and his old Balls, John Henry brought about his marriage with me, both of us the great grandchildren of the same pair—I, a thoughtless girl then staying at Earlham, and he nearly twice my age. But I don't blame them. Heaven knows their ignorance of my nature, and the utter want of congeniality in everything between his and me.

You know the ideal my heart and passions craved, and you know this reality circumstances and family considerations brought me; and you know from the day of that marriage I was silent. For when body and soul were in this, at last, both gone, I resolved to bear all patiently and submissively—to act and be the lie to the last. Indeed, as years wore on, it became almost my nature. I lost my inner light, as they say. I became a woman to look down from my social position and dwell in the proprieties forever.

There was then but one hope for me, and that hope was based upon the fact that I could not write to you. The pure, simple instincts of my girlhood, the ungratified passions, the real intelligence, lingered in me still. I dared not write to you—to you, who knew me so well, I dared not confess what my life had become. Yet more—I still had faith in my nature, because I felt I was silently degrading the crowning act of my mother's life by my weak and unnatural submission. I had faith over all when I first shrunk from the compliance with my vow, and when I prayed its living fruit might be in her image and not in mine. I felt then the force of nature *

Thus year after year passed away, and thus should I have lived and died; but I saw him, I heard his voice, I learned daily his thoughts, I revelled in his nature! Then I wrote to you again; my faith had become a living power; I began a new life.

Then came the fall, as ever before. The influence of social restraint was too terrible, and I sunk back as I did that day when we were children. This last assertion and denial of my nature brought me to the verge of death, but it brought me to reason also; and then, an altered being, weak and broken down, I rose, and with one fearful, silent struggle, that our sex's nature alone can know, I was forever free! Oh, the revelation of that hour! Life seemed in a moment no longer hard and difficult. Its relations were simple, its passions legitimate, its love supreme.

But let me narrate to you how I awakened to the reality of my position, my after experience, and how at last I had the strength to accomplish my emancipation.

The first few months of my married life I was truly not happy; but I cannot speak of that period as one of unhappiness. Indeed, during the whole spring I did not fully realize what that covenant means that disposes finally of the life of a woman, and that, too, at a time before the meaning of her nature consciously asserts itself. The novelty of the change, the new interests arising, the necessity to be a wife—all these feelings and emotions shut out myself from myself. And so it went on, month after month, in which I cannot recall anything that awakened me fully to the reality of my position.

But, E * * *, it was ordered in my life that it should come, and it came. A simple incident defined to me the meaning of my vow.

Among our visits to Earlham was one we made on the first day of the following autumn. I remember the date and the appearance of the country well. I shall never forget either. The fields were undulating with their golden grain. Costessy Park was in its fullest verdure. Everything seemed rejoicing in the coming harvest—the happy maternity of earth. And so we reached Earlham.

The first object I saw was Anna's child. It impressed me profoundly. I took him in my arms, and as I looked at him everything grew dark about me. I had been before the toy of a ceremony; I was now a conscious wife. Beautiful lawn and woodland, summer breezes, kindness, marriage rites even, what can they avail against the first awakening consciousness of a crime against nature?

I was wholly without sympathy; there were none around me to understand me. If I had spoken my thought the very air would have been filled with condemnation. I, a wife, had I a right to entertain for an instant such an idea? Could I dare to experience an instinct of aversion? Had I a right to say I had been violated—that I was what all women loathe?

I could not understand it; yet there it remained, a fact of my nature, asserting itself against the condition in which I was placed, and from which apparently no earthly power existed to release me.

I returned to Easton an altered being; but this feeling wore off somewhat in the routine, and in the necessities of married life—for his father's death, occurring shortly after, you remember, involved many changes and responsibilities, which turned, in a measure, for a time, the current of my thoughts.

Afterwards succeeded, at constantly recurring intervals of a year or two, many other deaths in our families which tended to check my free indulgence of thought, till at last my feelings settled simply into a sense of a vague but awful responsibility of a violation of the social law.

You must recall the constant distress and trouble into which we were all plunged by the successive deaths of his sister Anna, his aunt Catharine, my father and the children. The family at I—— Hall, too, was a weight which never ceased to press upon my heart, and, indeed, upon my whole existence.

And so I lived, but not among the living. I had my inner life and my outward life—what, I doubt not, other women have had as well as this poor one at Catton. I drummed, in the old school-girl way, into my husband's ears the set tunes for the piano, utterly unobservant of the music. I dressed in the same mechanical way to receive his relations, and thanked God when they were gone—and so underwent, beneath a conjugal yoke of continued kindness, a slow death. I entered into the life around me as an actress, real herself only when away from the stage of her action. I became the same that other women become, who turn from human faces to brute things for comfort. My early passion for horses and dogs proved then my consolation. I had to the full that mental nervousness which craves allayment in action. It would be impossible to admire a horse more than I had always done. It was an instinct of my nature, just as of Landseer's, or of old Mary Breeze's, of glorious memory; but I loved them now, for they were so much to me!

But when alone, immured, away from every one, I lived my fullest life. My imagination went away boldly, admiringly, lovingly, to other men. They were not objects of jealousy, dear E * * *, for they were dead.

I lived with the memories of the founders of our family—men who never sat upon the clerk's stool, and could never have claimed the benefit of clergy—men with strong arms and stalwart frames, making their deeds of knightly prowess known in a hundred battles—with the memories of Hugh, and Walter, and Anselm, and Girard, and Reginald, and Matthew and John, who in the Holy Land fought at Prince Edward's side, and rendered their red cross a terror to the Paynim. And my memory, only too tenacious, as you know, kept each noble form before me, with all the vividness of a present reality.

I lived with them, too, in their pastimes, in which—side by side with the Black Prince, in the eyes of their sovereign, and their gracious mistress, his Queen Phillippa, at the tournaments, held on the very spots where I daily rode—they mimicked their glorious achievements upon the veritable fields of blood which they had won.

I admired their splendid force, their brains not emasculate with such education as I saw around me, nor hampered with narrow trade tricks. I wondered what work they would be about if they were living to-day. I tried to imagine how any of the family could have got down, step by step, generation after generation, to studying Greek verbs, or calculating per cents.

Hugo alive, I knew well, would not be a praying banker, but abroad in the free air, adventuring crusades, simply and naturally, in whatever way the time demanded, just as the man I love, simply and naturally, and yet so irresistibly, rescued the sepulchre of my buried hopes and desires, against the law and the power, the ignorance and the infidelity to human nature, of all around me. All things great are simple. In the crusades my ancestors adventured, they went a long way across the world. It was as far as the distance between groom and lady, but not further. They conquered what was their own by right of their nature and their belief, and with such a struggle as every one must undergo who undertakes the assertion of his right against social law.

They conquered theirs as he did also his own; and does not his seem an act like, or nobler, than theirs? Is the rescue of a dead body a worthier act than the rescue of a living soul?

It was not so hard a conquest. My requirements were simple and natural. I was surrounded by everything unreal and artificial. I demanded the society of a living man, free from the education and influences of a family holding all these foolish theories that deprive us of the real enjoyments of life—one who could look upon water as water, and drink it without a homily—look upon food, not as a subject of prayer, but of mastication—enjoy the sunshine and air as sunshine and air, and talk with men and women as such without shrinking from them as heterodox, or loving them as orthodox too well—one who could listen to music and find it pleasant to the ear, and not be exercised whether God intended it should be agreeable—who could contemplate a picture not as an engine of the devil, but a work of art—one who could enjoy all delights as requirements of nature, and not as subjects of a deep concern. In Mr. Taylor I found such a man. He looked upon all these things as, indeed, I also saw them; but with him it was not a matter which cost him questioning. He knew it all without thought, and without education, as they call it. He lived in the intuitive knowledge of it.

In the interchange of kindred thoughts about these things we lived day by day, until, unconsciously, I found myself craving every word he spoke. I found his presence, which took me back to the men of my ancestral pride, a necessity of my life, and, at last, I felt myself for the first time beneath an influence of love.

The night that followed this discovery, when I knelt down by my bedside, his image stood between me and the far-off height on which my subjected brain had placed God.

And when I saw him there, I struggled, as I had been led to believe was duty, to dash down the image that stood at once in the way of my human vows and in the very presence of the stern methodical God of their education.

Yet there it stood, and there it must stand forever. Yes, dear E * * *, I loved him almost before I knew it; and he I felt, moreover, loved me, though not a word was spoken between us. It was not his to speak, and I would have concealed from my very inmost self the fact of this love.

But it could not be so forever. To maintain the form of a superiority, where none existed, became at last an impossibility. We loved, and the expression of it I foresaw could no longer be controlled by either, and so it came first from my lips. He was riding beside me, and did not reply to me. He said, out into the air, into the heavens: God has given me too great a joy. Then he turned to me and said: I have loved you from the first day I saw you. I loved you because I felt it was my destiny; other than this I know not why; I only know I loved you.

Dear E * * *, he was so beautiful, so noble then, in the expression of that love so long concealed. The earth whirled around me, and his arm caught me falling unconsciously. When I came to myself I was resting on his bosom, confident of its strength as of a breastplate of iron, though I saw his eyes dim with tears.

We rode homewards in silence. There was a beauty in the very stones beneath our feet. The wayside flowers had an odor too exquisite to the sense. The air and sky were filled with an influence too beautiful for earth. I was very, very happy. Could this feeling have rested in me, I had been content—faithful to my duty, as I had been taught—to have lived ever so. But my heart was now craving constantly the repetition of that moment. It could not be satisfied but in his presence. Hitherto patient only under a sense of wrong, I now began to be agitated by a passion in which every feeling of my life had centred.

It is not necessary to recount all the conflicts which it brought to me, nor to trace the way in which my nobler nature sunk gradually before the threatened penalty of social destruction; it is enough to say that I was borne by it to the decision which involved my destiny, and I yielded to the social law for the last time, because I had not yet come to that point at which a woman, driven to the very presence of death by the pressure of a false relation, thinks at last for herself, and hesitates no longer how to shape her course, should even the remaining wreck of her life be dashed to destruction.

Last autumn I began to feel myself breaking down. I could live thus no longer. When the time came we usually went to London, a while before the opening of Parliament, I felt that the crisis had come. If I went down with my husband in any hope of escaping the feelings that were mastering me, I knew well that on my return this life of passion would only recommence at sight of its object. If I remained alone, I believed I had strength to put it from me—I believed I could part with him, if for the days or weeks that would follow, after I had left him, I might meet no other gaze than God's—if I might exhaust the despair that I well knew would follow in silence.

I remained, therefore, at home.

I was not deceived in myself. The artificial being they had created of me was strong enough to assert itself and to sacrifice the love that lay in my heart's depths—but not till the last moment. It was only upon the very brink of my husband's return, that, arousing myself from the brief dream of happiness into which, secure in his absence, I had weakly fallen, I could summon the energy to take the draught of agony which, I believed, the hand of duty had prepared for me.

But further delay was now impossible.

I had him come to me. My heart was like a cup overrunning; my grief knew no expression. He was before me, at my feet. I cannot describe—no one dares acknowledge what passes between lovers, sundered by a social law; it is not possible to express that life within life, the innermost, the last.

I have brought you to me, I said, because I can see you no longer—I am dying.

My God, it seemed to me then as if my heart would break—as if I should go mad!

A moan of agony came to his lips.

He looked up at me; the intelligence of his face was gone; his eyes were dim; the despair that was in me changed his face to stone.

I looked on him immovably; I could say to him: We must part forever. I could repeat again the phrases of social life: There can be no honorable recognition of our love—its open avowal will bring disgrace to my husband and odium upon my children.

And how did he reply to me? Shall I confess, even there, in that hour of my strength, my utter weakness! I longed for a pleading word. One look of tenderness, and I should have fallen at his feet a ruined being, but ruined in the acknowledgment and utter abandon of my love.

Well he knew all this; but in that crisis he was true to himself, and to me; and when he ceased speaking, I was again strong. My head, my heart, every instinct of my being, approved his words, his looks, his actions.

He had saved me. He, as I knew him in that hour, was my strength; through him I conquered myself. I was strong in that final trial, as a woman only can be strong—through the soul and heart of the man who stands steadfast to himself and to her to the bitter end.

He said: Even in this hour, when every hope and joy of life have sunk away into eternal despair beneath your words, I can be true to my sense of right; I believe life requires no sacrifice; I believe self-sacrifice wrongs not only her who, blindly, in its belief as right, accepts it, but those the more for whom it is accepted. If, with your sense of duty, you were to sever the relation which binds you to them, it could bring you no happiness; its severance, as you feel, would bring at last misery to both, for your happiness is mine. There is no rule, no duty in life, but the pursuit of happiness. Mine can alone be purchased now at the cost of your own, and that is mine. We must part, then, forever!

The utter despair of these words can never leave my heart.

There were many things he said in this last interview which I recall, but it matters not now should be repeated. Our lives express them more clearly than words. He spoke of the false relation which he had gradually been led to assume, and into the continuance of which our passion had held him day by day.

I knew well, he said, it should long ago have been terminated; but I knew not then, as now, the controlling power that has kept me by you until this hour. I believed, first, that I might love you, and that you might remain forever unconscious of my love. And so I lived till this was impossible. And then my life became one eternal delay of hope, enduring all to this last measure of despair. It could not be otherwise. I believed from day to day that you would see clearly, as I saw, the right, and so it might at last end. It is over now! My life is over. My lot is hopeless, endless misery. I accept it for your sake—for the memory of our love.

Then my life, my very soul, met his in one long kiss of agony, and we parted, as I believed, forever.

I had conquered my life; this social law had achieved its triumph.

When my husband reached home I was strong to do the last duty which my position imposed upon me. I knew well that, cost what it would, this must also be done. I must live the life, to which I was bound, openly. I went to him and told him of my love, of my resolution, and of our separation. Much passed between us at this horrible time; but all that was in my heart to say was just these words: I love William. Of the rest, and of what followed, I have no clear remembrance.

I only knew now that he must be gone—that life, hope, all were gone, though I remained there still that honorable thing, a wife! For me, it was determined that I should leave England for a time. I was to travel. A change of scene they prescribed for the invalid of the heart. It was always the same, the same ignorance of a woman's nature and its necessities. They would have me enjoy Paris, Rome. They would substitute the splendor of the Vatican for some little flower that might perchance come from his hand should I remain at home. It seemed so much more to them.

Absorbed in the contemplation of the ruins of my life, I took no heed of these arrangements for my departure, but abandoned myself a willing prey to despair.

When the full measure of my grief had exhausted itself, I arose a new being.

From that moment I was myself. I had driven every hope, every feeling from my heart. I had received from his lips the last sacrifice a man can offer to the woman he loves—the abnegation of himself for her happiness; and I declare before Heaven that it was my resolve to do what I thought right, though it cost me my life; for I had nothing now to live for.

I had long followed blindly a passion that brought me to the verge of social destruction. I had renounced it.

I had blindly followed for years a path of duty which had degraded every instinct of my nature to its last measure of degradation.

I could feel no more—I reasoned.

The meaning of the life I was about to enter upon was now distinctly before me. What it appeared to me, I well knew it was, in very reality, for I was now freed from my love. I had sacrificed all for duty. I could see now to what the blind obedience of that duty had led me. What I was I now knew.

My soul was clear from hypocrisy—there was not any lie upon it now. I had confessed all. My very life was laid open to my heart's core. My love was gone, as well by his will as my own, forever.

What had I accomplished? I had preserved the chaste name of wife. I had preserved the honor of my husband and the reputation of his children. And to do it, I was beneath his roof, and was about to submit myself to his embraces without love.

For these considerations of honor and reputation, I was about to lead voluntarily a life of prostitution, distinguished from it only by the social fiction of a name, and I felt myself more degraded for all this honorable hire than she who accepts her paltry dole in the streets.

I was, moreover, about to fulfil functions from which every fibre of my body shrunk with abhorrence. I was there to give life to offspring created in my own degradation, in violation of my will and nature, the effete offspring of blood kin, children to die feebly before their time, or perhaps to come into the world, they, or their children, deformed, or dumb, or blind, or imbecile. I, who was perfect myself, and formed to receive and transmit the sacred treasure of a new life, was to become voluntarily the matricide of the more perfect conceptions which should be mine.

Better, in the agony of that thought, I said, better death than this—better self-immolation of body and soul; it were far less a crime.

And then, shuddering with horror upon the brink to which duty had led me, I supplicated my soul imploringly for light, as I asked myself the great question: Does any law of God sanction, shall any law of man have the power to continue, the bond of marriage where no love exists?

And I answered it, as my children, if they inherit aught of my nature, shall at last approve, as the world shall at last come to understand.

Thus was I at once and forever severed from all former relations and left alone in the world.

I write these last words quietly, here at my writing desk; but that inquisition of my brain, it was terrible—more terrible even than the death I had accepted in parting from him.

But my decision was made, and I was calm then.

I knew in that moment the rest of a fearful struggle of the brain—the poor weak brain of a woman—that swept the world, though, beneath her feet.

There was grief in that family, when I became in that decision myself, and stood a stranger among them; when the social fabric, his children, their father, false pride, conventional position—all had overthrow; when my mother's wrongs had revenge, and my father's love had justification, in the child of his life-wronged wife!

But their grief was joy to the agony of calm in which I made that decision.

Not a tear came to my eye when I told it them; not a pulse stirred in my breast. How inconceivable to them all this agony.

My husband was even still solicitous to preserve the form of a union, now no longer possible in reality. One of those formality doctors of the soul was sent for—his uncle Francis. O! after all the agony I had passed through, I might have been spared the sight of one of those whose words had sanctioned and stamped upon me, as if by the authority of God, all this misery.

But how weak and idle to me were his words about theological sin and social infamy. They fell on my ear, in constant repetition, meaningless as the dropping of the beads of a rosary.

He told me I was imperiling my soul, and he left me with some formal expression of pious horror, when I told him I would willingly incur that risk.

And now I was alone in the world—my life still before me—severed from every living relation—to be lived or ended. What new connections must I assume? Unsupported, helpless, alone, where should I go? What must I do?

In those past ages the convent doors would have been open to me; but my intelligence, the intelligence of the very age in which I lived, forbade me the immolation of my living body and my free soul.

And then came to me again the idea of suicide.

I did not shrink from this thought superstitiously, as fearing to rush unbidden into the presence of the offended deities. I had no such thought. It meant to me only rest from this great burden and weariness of life—to lie down and sleep while it was yet day—to sleep forever.

But I was too calm for the rashness of this act—too strong. If they, who retired to the cloister from a sense of a superstitious duty, willingly endured its burden, I, with larger intelligence, could not sink beneath their lower thought, and weakly die. No, I had committed no crime that I should die; nor were my past misfortunes a reason why I should voluntarily impose new ones upon my life to come. I knew I was in the world to live. Vigor of body, of mind, passions, desires, reason, all that goes to make up a human soul, were in the full tide of existence; and I was here surely not to contemplate death, but to fulfil the functions of life—of a new life.

For I had absolutely died in that decision to live free from my bond. I was dead to all past relations and connections. I was dead to the social world around me, as if I had never lived before. The consciousness of my identity was gone. Every eye rested strangely upon me. I was as a child new born. I would have put out my hands simply as a child, for I was in the living world, again, a stranger; new born, with a life in perfect maturity.

And so came the final question:——

Shall the right I have asserted to live apart from my husband be followed by cutting off every desire, by marring or concealing every beauty, by devoting the remainder of a life, already cursed by an involuntary indiscretion of youth, to asceticism, and so continue in another form the struggle against nature to the end?——or accept the creed of the man I love, and seek also my highest happiness in the gratification of that love, which every instinct of my being approves?

And my answer to this final question is before you and all the world.

As I said at first, dear, I have no misgivings about the sincerity of your affection for me, under any changes of life; and I feel just as sure that you will never doubt the constant, undying friendship of

Your

LITTLE MARY.

TO MRS. ——,

LONDON.

———